HOLIDAY ORIGAMI

Thanksgiving
Origami

by Ruth Owen

PowerKiDS
press™

New York

Published in 2013 by The Rosen Publishing Group, Inc.
29 East 21st Street, New York, NY 10010

Produced for Rosen by Ruby Tuesday Books Ltd
Editor for Ruby Tuesday Books Ltd: Mark J. Sachner
US Editor: Sara Antill
Designer: Emma Randall

Photo Credits:
Cover, 1, 3, 5, 7, 9 (top right), 12 (bottom right), 16 (top right), 20 (top left), 21 (top right), 24 (bottom left), 28 (bottom left) © Shutterstock.
Origami models © Ruby Tuesday Books Ltd.

Library of Congress Cataloging-in-Publication Data

Owen, Ruth, 1967–
Thanksgiving origami / by Ruth Owen.
      p. cm. — (Holiday origami)
Includes index.
ISBN 978-1-4488-7864-2 (library binding) — ISBN 978-1-4488-7923-6 (pbk.) — ISBN 978-1-4488-7929-8 (6-pack)
1. Origami—Juvenile literature. 2. Thanksgiving decorations—Juvenile literature. I. Title.
TT870.O956 2013
736'.982—dc23

2012009648

Manufactured in the United States of America

CPSIA Compliance Information: Batch # B4S12PK: For Further Information contact Rosen Publishing, New York, New York at 1-800-237-9932

Contents

Origami in Action

Have you ever heard of **origami**? Origami is the art of folding paper to make small models, or **sculptures**.

Some kinds of sculptures, such as those made from wood or stone, can last for hundreds of years. Paper does not last that long, though. For that reason, we do not know when people first began making origami models.

We do know, though, that origami has been popular for centuries in Japan. In fact, "origami" is Japanese for "folding paper."

If you've never tried origami before, don't worry! This book will take you step-by-step through some fun Thanksgiving projects, such as turkeys, apples, and even corn on the cob! So get some paper and start folding!

Get Folding!

Before you get started on your Thanksgiving origami models, here are some tips.

Tip 1
Read all the instructions carefully and look at the pictures. Make sure you understand what's required before you begin a fold. Don't rush, but be patient. Work slowly and carefully.

Tip 2
Folding a piece of paper sounds easy, but it can be tricky to get neat, accurate folds. The more you practice, the easier it becomes.

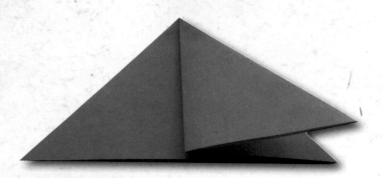

Tip 3
If an instruction says "crease," make the crease as flat as possible. The flatter the creases, the better the model. You can make a sharp crease by running a plastic ruler along the edge of the paper.

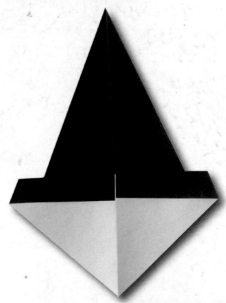

Tip 4
Sometimes, at first, your models may look a little crumpled. Don't give up! The more models you make, the better you will get at folding and creasing.

When it comes to origami, practice makes perfect!

Just take a look at these origami flowers made by an experienced model maker. Keep practicing and you could become an origami master!

One of the most common origami models made in Japan is a type of bird called a crane.

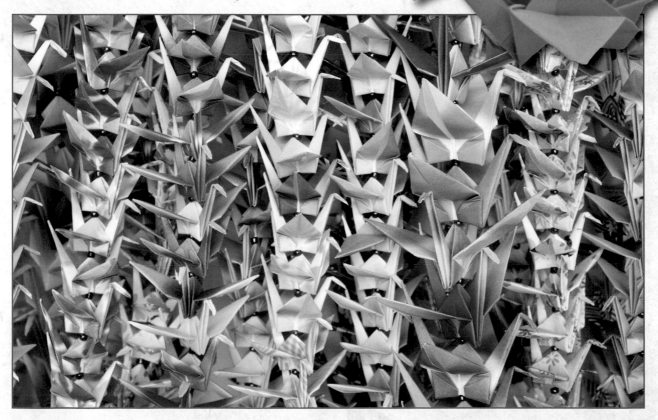

People in Japan say that if you fold 1,000 paper cranes, all your wishes will come true. Sometimes people make 1,000 cranes to give as a gift to a person who is unwell, or to a couple about to get married.

Origami Pilgrim

In 1620, a group of English settlers landed in Plymouth Harbor, in what would later become the state of Massachusetts. The **colony** they **founded** would become one of the first successful English settlements in North America.

The **Pilgrims** faced incredible hardships, and many of their group didn't survive the first winter. With the help of native Wampanoag people, however, the Pilgrims planted crops, and by the fall of 1621, they had a bountiful harvest. To give thanks for their good fortune, the Pilgrims held a feast with their Wampanoag neighbors. That feast is recreated every year on Thanksgiving Day!

To make the pilgrim, you will need:

Two sheets of black origami paper

Colored pencils

Peel and stick googly eyes

(Origami paper is sometimes colored on both sides or white on one side.)

STEP 1:
Place the paper colored side down. Fold the paper diagonally, and crease.

STEP 2:
Fold both sides into the center along the dotted lines, and crease.

STEP 3:
Fold the bottom half of the model up along the dotted line, and crease.

STEP 4:
Now fold the top layer of paper back down toward you along the dotted line, and crease.

STEP 5:
Your model should now look like this.

STEP 6:
Flip your model over. Fold in on the two dotted lines, and crease. These are tricky folds to make!

STEP 7:
The back of your model should look like this.

STEP 8:
This next part is tricky. Gently pull the little pockets at A and B outward and flatten.

A   B

STEP 9:
The back of your model should now look like this.

STEP 10:
Fold the top and bottom points, and crease.

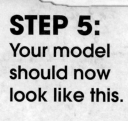

STEP 11:

Turn the model over. Use a pink pencil to draw the pilgrim's chin over his collar. Color the face pink and give him googly eyes and a mouth.

STEP 12:

To make the pilgrim's body, repeat steps 1 and 2.

STEP 13:

Fold up the bottom point and crease.

STEP 14:

Fold down the top point so that it overlaps the bottom point.

STEP 15:

Now make two folds along the dotted lines.

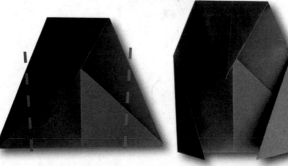

STEP 16:

Tuck the top of the body under the back of the pilgrim's hat. Unfold parts C and D, and your pilgrim should be able to stand.

C   D

Origami Turkey

In the 1500s, Spanish soldiers returned to Europe with turkeys that people in Mexico had been breeding for thousands of years. When early settlers came to North America, they brought some of this breed with them. Little did they know that relatives of these turkeys had been a favorite food of native people in North America for centuries!

While we don't know for sure if turkey was eaten at the first Thanksgiving, today it is a central part of the feast. Every year, about 45 million turkeys are served at Thanksgiving dinners across the United States!

To make origami turkeys you will need:

One sheet of paper for each turkey. Be creative and make turkeys in different colors!

(Origami paper is sometimes colored on both sides or white on one side.)

A

STEP 1:
Place the paper colored side down. Fold the paper diagonally, and crease.

STEP 2:
Fold both sides into the center along the dotted lines, and crease.

STEP 3:
Fold down point A and tuck inside the model.

STEP 4:
Now fold points B and C behind the model.

B   C

The front of the model will look like this.

The back of the model will look like this.

STEP 5:
Unfold both corners.

13

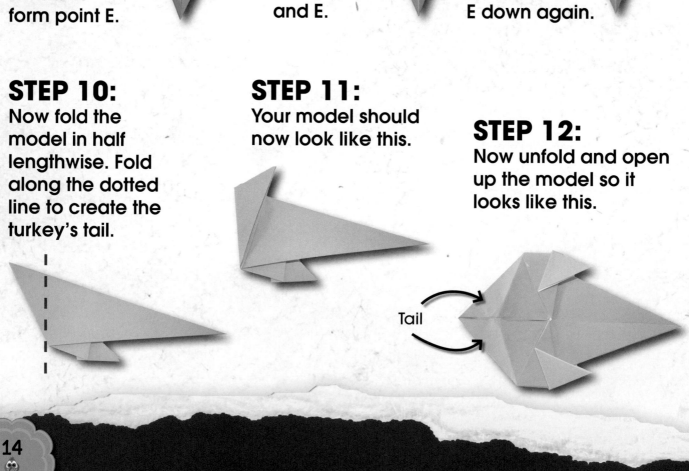

STEP 6:
This next part is tricky! Unfold the left side of the model. Then collapse the paper back down to form point D.

STEP 7:
Repeat on the right side of the model to form point E.

STEP 8:
Fold up points D and E.

STEP 9:
Now fold points D and E down again.

STEP 10:
Now fold the model in half lengthwise. Fold along the dotted line to create the turkey's tail.

STEP 11:
Your model should now look like this.

STEP 12:
Now unfold and open up the model so it looks like this.

Tail

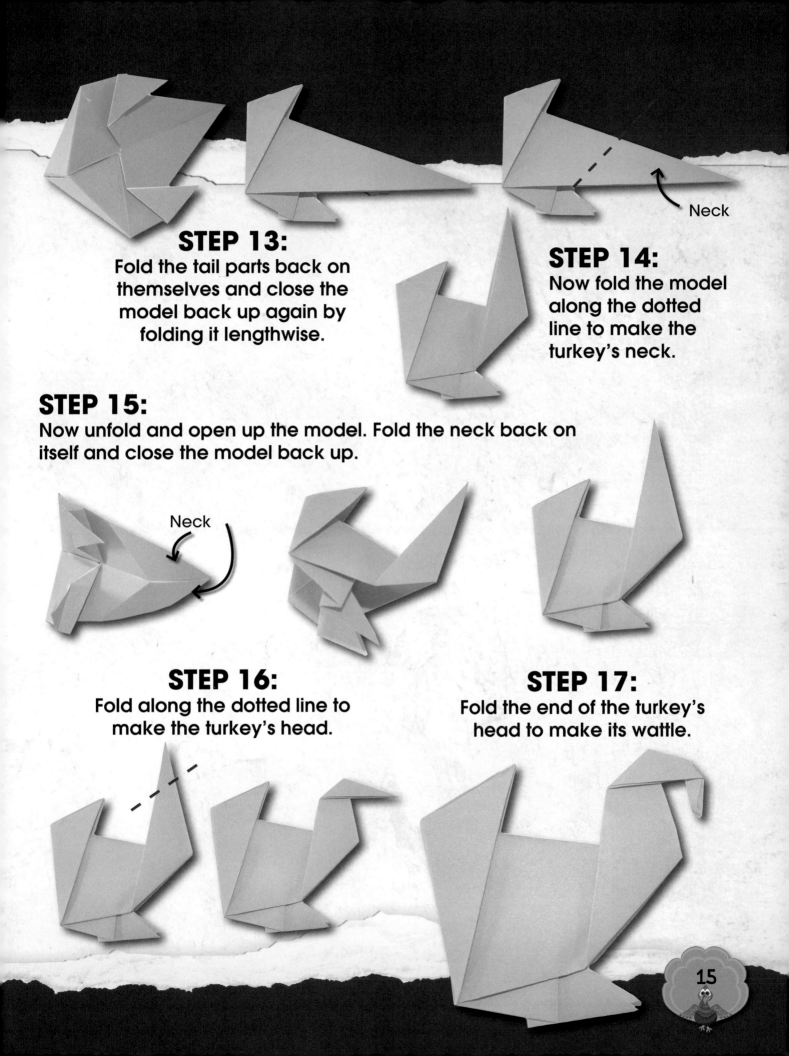

Neck

STEP 13:
Fold the tail parts back on themselves and close the model back up again by folding it lengthwise.

STEP 14:
Now fold the model along the dotted line to make the turkey's neck.

STEP 15:
Now unfold and open up the model. Fold the neck back on itself and close the model back up.

Neck

STEP 16:
Fold along the dotted line to make the turkey's head.

STEP 17:
Fold the end of the turkey's head to make its wattle.

Origami Pumpkins

Pumpkins and squashes had been grown by Native Americans for over 5,000 years. Their connection with Thanksgiving comes right from the story of the first Thanksgiving feast, where pumpkin was probably served alongside deer meat and corn.

Today, from pumpkins sold at roadside stands to slices of rich pumpkin pie served at Thanksgiving, pumpkins are all about autumn, the harvest, and feeling warm indoors when it's getting cold outside. Make origami pumpkins and squashes in orange, yellow, and green to create a festive Thanksgiving decoration.

To make origami pumpkins and squashes you will need:

Sheets of orange, green, and yellow origami paper

(Origami paper is sometimes colored on both sides or white on one side.)

STEP 1:
Place the paper colored side down. Fold the paper diagonally and crease.

STEP 2:
Fold the triangle you've made in half again, and crease.

STEP 3:
Now take corner A and fold back along the dotted line.

A

STEP 4:
Take hold of corner A and lift up. Then open up the pocket. Check that what you have looks like this picture.

A   Pocket

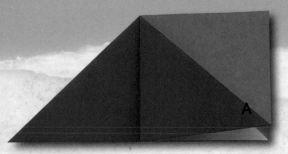

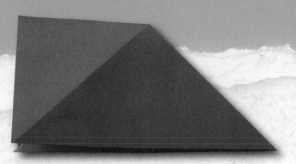

STEP 5:

Now gently squash down the pocket so it collapses to form a square.

STEP 6:

Flip your model over so it looks like this.

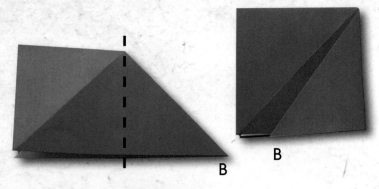

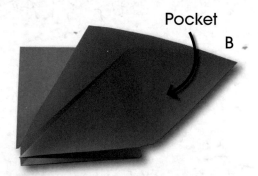

Pocket

STEP 7:

Now take corner B and fold it back along the dotted line. (You should now have a square shape.)

STEP 8:

Take hold of corner B, lift, and open up the pocket. Check that what you have looks like this picture.

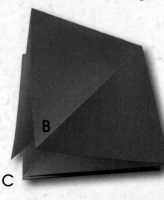

STEP 9:

Now, gently push down on corner B and the model should collapse so that corner B meets corner C. Check that your model is a square shape.

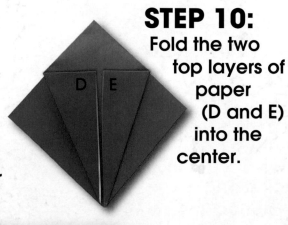

STEP 10:

Fold the two top layers of paper (D and E) into the center.

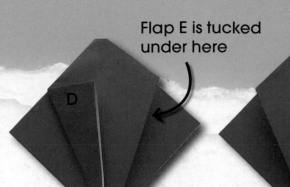

Flap E is tucked under here

D

F G

STEP 11:
Now tuck flaps D and E under themselves.

STEP 12:
Fold in the two top edges F and G.

STEP 13:
Now tuck flaps F and G under themselves.

STEP 14:
Fold the top and bottom points behind the model, and crease well.

STEP 15:
Fold the two sides behind the model, and crease well. You can make your pumpkin thinner or fatter by changing where you make the final four folds.

Origami Ears of Corn

Like pumpkins and turkey, corn has been an all-American food for thousands of years. In Mexico and Central America, ancient **civilizations** traded corn centuries before Europeans even knew the Americas existed.

Over those centuries, the growing of corn spread throughout North and South America. By the time of the first Thanksgiving in 1621, one of the gifts the Pilgrims celebrated was the successful harvest of corn as taught by their Wampanoag neighbors. Today, corn is as much a part of the feast itself as it was nearly four hundred years ago!

To make ears of corn you will need:

One sheet of yellow origami paper and
one sheet of green for each ear of corn

A black marker

(Origami paper is sometimes colored on both sides or white on one side.)

STEP 1:
To make the
green corn
husk, place
the paper
colored side down.
Fold the paper diagonally,
and crease.

STEP 2:
Fold both sides into
the center along the
dotted lines, and
crease.

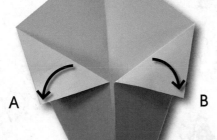

STEP 3:
Fold down points
A and B

STEP 4:
Now fold points A
and B back up again.

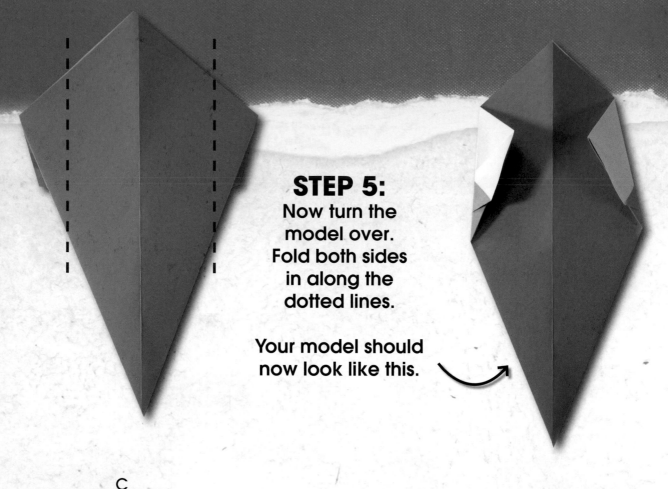

STEP 5:

Now turn the model over. Fold both sides in along the dotted lines.

Your model should now look like this.

C

STEP 6:

Now fold point C down and point D up.

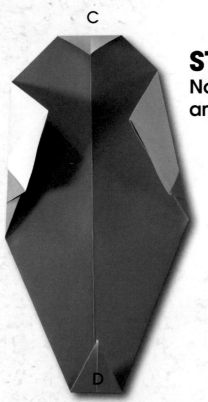

D

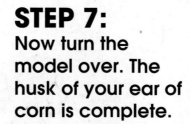

STEP 7:

Now turn the model over. The husk of your ear of corn is complete.

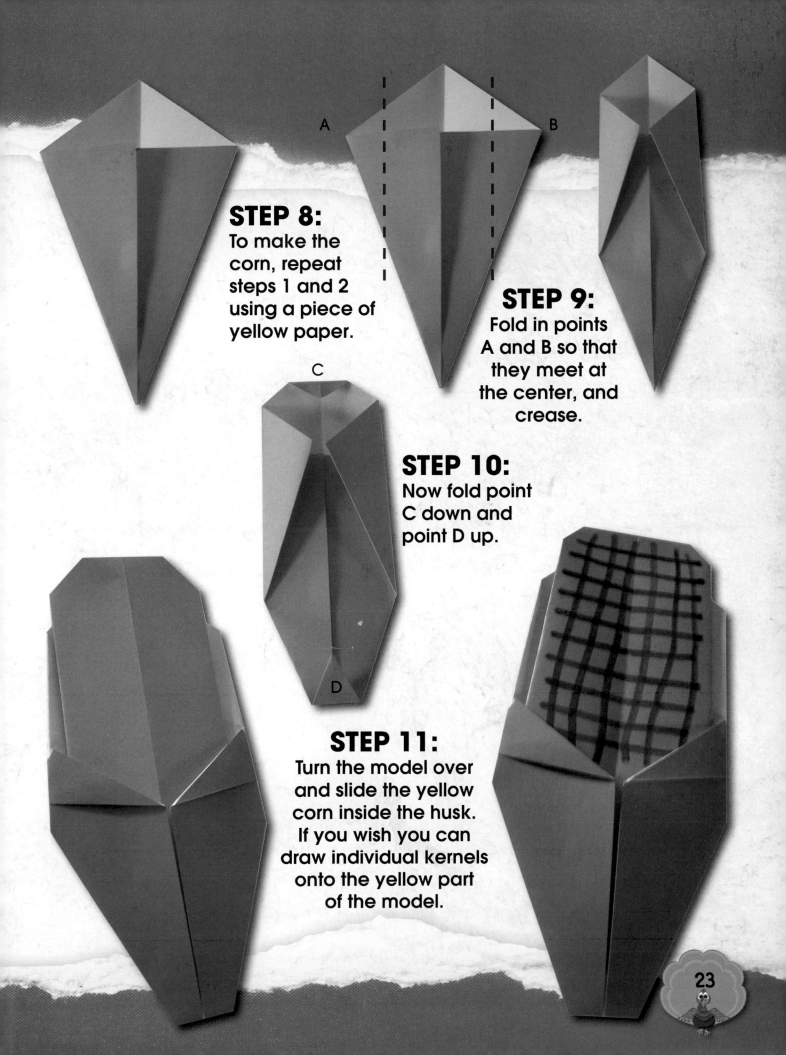

STEP 8:

To make the corn, repeat steps 1 and 2 using a piece of yellow paper.

A

B

STEP 9:

Fold in points A and B so that they meet at the center, and crease.

C

STEP 10:

Now fold point C down and point D up.

D

STEP 11:

Turn the model over and slide the yellow corn inside the husk. If you wish you can draw individual kernels onto the yellow part of the model.

Origami Apple Harvest

One of the symbols of Thanksgiving is the **cornucopia**, or "horn of plenty," It is a horn-shaped basket filled with fruits and vegetables from a successful harvest.

The "horn of plenty" dates back to the days of the ancient Greeks and Romans. They used the symbol of a goat's horn overflowing with fruits, flowers, and grains to represent an **abundance** of food and good luck.

Like pumpkins and corn, apples are harvested in the fall. So make this crop of colorful origami apples. Then add it to your pumpkins, squashes, and ears of corn, to have your own abundant harvest, or cornucopia, of Thanksgiving origami foods.

To make apples, you will need:

Sheets of red and green origami paper

(Origami paper is sometimes colored on both sides or white on one side.)

STEP 1:
Place the paper colored side down. Fold the paper diagonally, and crease.

STEP 2:
Fold both sides into the center along the dotted lines, so that each side reaches just over the center fold. The two sides will overlap.

STEP 3:
Fold down the top point.

25

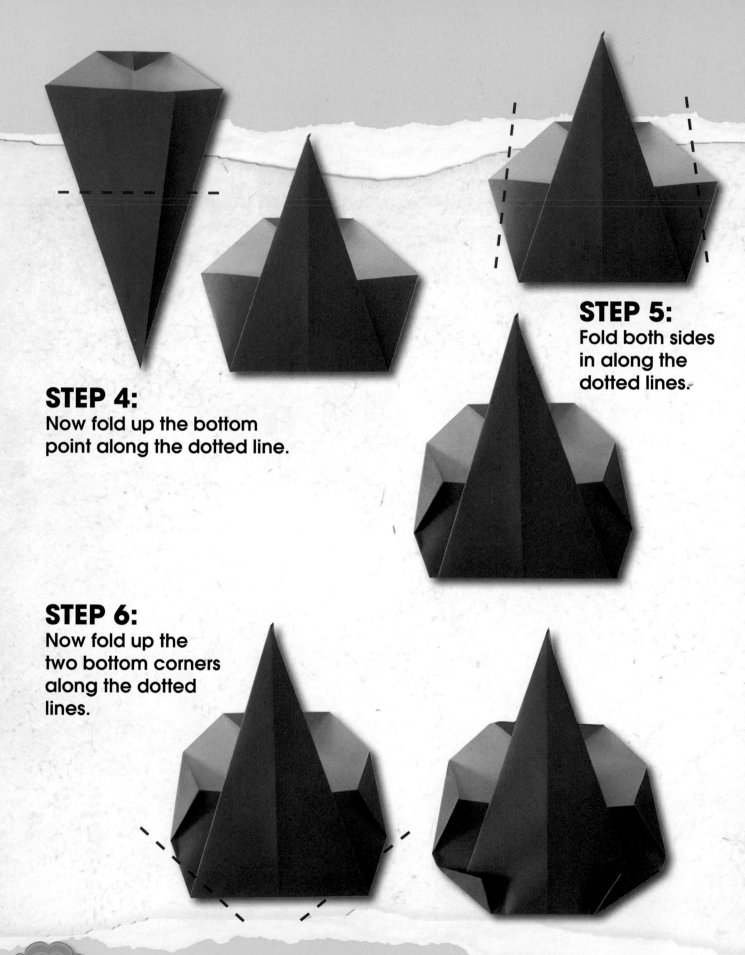

STEP 4:
Now fold up the bottom point along the dotted line.

STEP 5:
Fold both sides in along the dotted lines.

STEP 6:
Now fold up the two bottom corners along the dotted lines.

STEP 7:
Turn the model over. It should look like this.

STEP 8:
Fold down the top point to make the apple's stem.

STEP 9:
Now you have everything you need to create a Thanksgiving origami harvest display!

Origami Autumn Leaves

In much of North America, nature has a beautiful way of leading us out of summer—the turning of autumn leaves from green to brilliant shades of red, yellow, and orange. And when the leaves turn brown and fall to the ground, they ease us into the darkness and cold of winter.

The colors of autumn leaves belong to Thanksgiving, too. They are nature's way of celebrating the harvest. Even some of our favorite Thanksgiving foods, such as cranberries, corn, sweet potatoes, and pumpkin pie, are perfectly matched to the colors of autumn!

To make autumn leaves you will need:

Sheets of origami paper in reds, yellows, oranges, and browns

(Origami paper is sometimes colored on both sides or white on one side).

STEP 1:
Place the paper colored side down. Fold the paper diagonally, and crease.

STEP 2:
Fold the top and bottom points into the center fold, and crease.

STEP 3:
Fold the model in half.

STEP 4:
Make a fold at one end of the model.

STEP 5:
Now turn the model over and make a fold in the other direction. Use the first fold as a marker for the size of the second folded part.

STEP 6:
Turn the model back over and make another fold. Keep turning and folding.

STEP 7:
When all the paper is folded, your model should look like this.

STEP 8:
Take hold of both ends of the model and gently pull in opposite directions to open out the folds.

STEP 9:
Gently open out the model.
It should look like a leaf!

STEP 10:
Squeeze together the end of
the model where you began
folding to make a stem.

Stem

STEP 11:
Make autumn leaves in a range of colors. You can
scatter them over your Thanksgiving dinner table to
make fantastic seasonal table decorations.

Glossary

abundance (uh-BUN-dens) Plenty; a very large quantity or number of something.

civilizations (sih-vih-lih-ZAY-shunz) Cultures or nations existing in a certain area and at a certain time.

colony (KAH-luh-nee) An area that is settled by people from another region and that is under the control of the country those people are from.

cornucopia (kor-nuh-KOH-pee-uh) A symbol of plenty or abundance consisting of a large horn filled with flowers, fruit, corn, and other plants.

founded (FOWN-did) Begun, started, or set up.

origami (or-uh-GAH-mee) The art of folding paper into decorative shapes or objects.

Pilgrims (PIL-grumz) Members of a group who came to America from England in search of religious freedom and founded the Plymouth Colony in present-day Massachusetts in 1620.

sculptures (SKULP-cherz) Works of art that have a shape to them, such as statues or carved objects, and may be made of wood, stone, metal, plaster, or even paper.

Index

Websites

Due to the changing nature of Internet links, PowerKids Press has developed an online list of websites related to the subject of this book. This site is updated regularly. Please use this link to access the list:
www.powerkidslinks.com/horig/thanks/